## Describe simple patterns and relationships involving numbers examples satisfy given conditions

## Describe ways of solving puzzles and problems, explaining choices and decisions orally or using pictures

Reprinted 2011, 2012
Published 2009 by A&C Black,
an imprint of Bloomsbury Publishing Plc
50 Bedford Square, London WC1B 3DP
www.acblack.com

ISBN 978-1-4081-1315-8

Copyright text © Hilary Koll and Steve Mills 2009
Copyright illustrations © Gaynor Berry 2009
Copyright cover illustration © Piers Baker 2009
Editors: Marie Lister
Designed by Billin Design Solutions Ltd

The authors and publishers would like to thank Catherine Yemm and Judith Wells for their advice in producing this series of books.

A CIP catalogue record for this book is available from the British Library.

Printed and bound in Great Britain by Caligraving.

A&C Black uses paper produced with elemental chlorine-free pulp, harvested from managed sustainable forests.

# Introduction

**100% New Developing Mathematics: Using and Applying Mathematics** is a series of seven photocopiable activity books for children aged 4 to 11, designed to be used during the daily maths lesson. The books focus on the skills and concepts for Using and Applying Mathematics as outlined in the Primary National Strategy *Primary Framework for literacy and mathematics*. The activities are intended to be used in the time allocated to pupil activities in the daily maths lesson. They aim to reinforce the knowledge and develop the skills and understanding explored during the main part of the lesson, and to provide practice and consolidation of the learning objectives contained in the Framework document.

## Using and Applying Mathematics

There are several different components which make up the content of maths and form the bulk of any maths curriculum:

- **mathematical facts**, for example a triangle has three sides;
- **mathematical skills**, such as counting;
- **mathematical concepts**, like place value.

For maths teaching to be successful, it is vital that children can use this mathematical content beyond their classroom, either in real-life situations or as a basis for further understanding. However, in order to do so they require extra abilities over and above the mathematical content they have learned. These extra abilities are often referred to as the **processes** of mathematical activity. It is these processes which make mathematical content usable.

As an example, consider this question:

*How many triangles are there in this shape?*

The mathematical 'content' required is only:

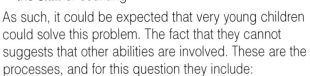

- the **fact** that a triangle has three sides
- the **skill** of counting

As such, it could be expected that very young children could solve this problem. The fact that they cannot suggests that other abilities are involved. These are the processes, and for this question they include:

- visualising the different-sized triangles;
- being systematic in counting all the triangles of different sizes;
- looking for patterns in the numbers of triangles;
- trial and error;
- recording.

Unless children can apply these processes in this situation, then however good their counting skills and knowledge of triangles may be, they will fail.

The strand 'Using and applying mathematics' of the *Primary Framework for mathematics* emphasises the importance of using and talking about the mathematics in real situations. This series of books is intended to make more explicit the processes involved in learning how to put one's maths to use.

**Using and Applying Mathematics Ages 5–6** supports the development of the using and applying processes by providing a series of activities that provide opportunities to introduce and practise them through a series of activities. On the whole the activities are designed for children to work on independently, although due to the young age of the children, the teacher may need to read the instructions with them and ensure that they understand the activity before they begin working on it.

Pre-school children are naturally inquisitive about the world around them. They like to explore and experiment, and to make marks and record things on paper in their own idiosyncratic ways. Once at school, the focus is often placed firmly on the maths 'content' alone and children can sometimes believe that maths is not a subject of exploration, but rather one of simply learning the 'right way to do things'. As a result, when older children are asked to explore and investigate maths they are often at a loss.

**Ages 5–6** helps children to develop the following processes:

- predicting
- visualising
- looking for pattern
- recording
- reasoning
- making decisions
- estimating
- explaining
- being systematic
- co-operating
- comparing
- testing ideas
- trial and improvement
- asking own question

When using these activities, the focus need not be on the actual mathematical 'content'. Instead, the teacher's demonstrations, discussions and questioning should emphasise the processes the children are using. When appropriate, invite the children to explain their thinking to others. Research has shown that children develop processes most successfully when the teacher encourages pupils to act as experts rather than novices, granting them more autonomy, and encouraging a range of approaches to any problem rather than constraining discussion to produce an overall class plan. The children should evaluate their own plans against other plans in the posing, planning and monitoring phases of the lessons.

**Ages 5–6** also helps children with Solving Problems, Representing, Enquiring, Reasoning and Communicating, as recommended in the revised Primary Framework. These five themes, although identified separately in the table below, are interlinked.

| Using and applying mathematics | Solving problems | Representing | Enquiring | Reasoning | Communicating |
|---|---|---|---|---|---|
| Year 1 | Solve problems involving counting, adding, subtracting, doubling or halving in the context of numbers, measures or money, for example to 'pay' and 'give change' | Describe a puzzle or problem using numbers, practical materials and diagrams; use these to solve the problem and set the solution in the original context | Answer a question by selecting and using suitable equipment, and sorting information, shapes or objects; display results using tables and pictures | Describe simple patterns and relationships involving numbers or shapes; decide whether examples satisfy given conditions | Describe ways of solving puzzles and problems, explaining choices and decisions orally or using pictures |

## Extension

Many of the activity sheets end with a challenge (**Now try this!**), which reinforces and extends children's learning, and provides the teacher with an opportunity for assessment. Again, it may be necessary to read the instructions with the children before they begin the activity. For some of the challenges the children will need to record their answers on a separate piece of paper.

## Organisation

Very little equipment is needed, but it will be useful to have the following resources available: coloured pencils, counters, interlocking cubes, scissors, real or plastic coins, paper, dice, dominoes, pencils in a pencil pot, numeral cards, cubes.

Where possible, the children's work should be supported by ICT equipment, such as number lines and tracks on interactive whiteboards, or computer software for comparing and ordering numbers. It is also vital that children's experiences are introduced in real-life contexts and through practical activities. The teachers' notes at the foot of each page and the more detailed notes on pages 6 to 13 suggest ways in which this can be done effectively.

To help teachers select appropriate learning experiences for the children, the activities are grouped into sections within the book. However, the activities are not expected to be used in this order unless stated otherwise. The sheets are intended to support, rather than direct, the teacher's planning.

Some activities can be made easier or more challenging by masking or substituting numbers. You may wish to re-use pages by copying them onto card and laminating them.

## Accompanying CD

The enclosed CD-ROM contains all of the activity sheets from the book and a program that allows you to edit them for printing or saving. This means that modifications can be made to further differentiate the activities to suit individual pupils' needs. See page 14 for further details.

## Teachers' notes

Brief notes are provided at the foot of each page, giving ideas and suggestions for maximising the effectiveness of the activity sheets. These can be masked before copying.

Solutions and further explanations of the activities can be found on pages 6 to 13, together with examples of questions that you can ask.

## Whole class warm-up activities

The following activities provide some practical ideas that can be used to introduce or reinforce the main teaching part of the lesson, or provide an interesting basis for discussion.

## Imagine my shape

Describe a 3D shape that you have hidden and ask the children to guess what shape it is, for example 'The shape has five faces. Four are triangles and one is a square.' Confirm suggested answers by using 3D shapes and counting sides, faces and corners.

## What's the star number?

This activity focuses on predicting missing numbers in a sequence. Draw circles on the board and a star and write several numbers into them, either counting on in ones, twos or fives, for example:

Children must predict the number in the star and to explain how they formed their opinion. Then check their predictions by counting on (or back).

## How many?

Ask questions like: 'How many steps is it from my table to the door?' 'How many handspans will fit across your table?' Discuss estimates and then count to check.

## Here's the answer

Write a number on the board, for example 12. Explain that this number is the answer to a calculation. Ask the children to come to the board and write a calculation with 12 as the answer, for example 9 + 3 or 14 – 2.

# Notes on the activities

**Solve problems involving counting, adding, subtracting, doubling or halving in the context of numbers, measures or money, for example to 'pay' and 'give change'**

This aspect of Using and Applying Mathematics deals with Solving Problems. It is central to all mathematics and if the children are unable to solve problems then the mathematics that they know is wasted. The children need to develop confidence in tackling problems without looking to teachers or other children for help. They should learn to decide which facts are key to the problem, make decisions about what operations to use and then follow them through, checking to see if their answer is a sensible one.

## Penguins (pages 15)

*Processes: make decisions, record, reason, explain*

Providing young children with choice about numbers is very important as maths is often introduced as fixed and inflexible. Here the children have a choice as to the number of penguins they choose to colour and from which ice-floes. Encourage them to check each other's work by counting those that are coloured. As an extension activity, ask the children to record each situation in some way using numbers then discuss these and invite them to say which approach is clearest and easiest to understand.

**SUGGESTED QUESTIONS:**

- Why did you choose this number?
- How many have you coloured here?
- How many have not been coloured?
- How could you write this for someone else to understand?

## Flapjacks (page16)

*Processes: visualise, make decisions, estimate, compare, ask own questions*

Encourage the children to think about the different lengths of flapjacks, to sort and organise them in different ways, and use appropriate vocabulary. Providing resources for the children to compare lengths can create many opportunities for questioning and comparing.

**SUGGESTED QUESTIONS:**

- How many flapjacks are about the same length as this one?
- Can you find a piece that is about half the length of this one?
- Can you find two pieces of flapjack that are about the same length as one other?

## At the shoe shop (page17)

*Processes: visualise, look for pattern, predict*

At the start of the lesson, draw sets of 6 shoes, 10 shoes, 14 shoes and 8 shoes on the board. Ask the children to say how many pairs are in each set and discuss how the children can use halving to work this out quickly. As a further extension activity, the children could predict how many pairs for 15, 17 shoes, and so on.

**SUGGESTED QUESTIONS:**

- How many shoes?
- How many pairs?
- How many left over?
- What is the largest number that could be left over? Why is this?

## Money, money (page18)

*Processes: record, reason, compare, be systematic*
*Begin by discussing possible coins that could be used.*

**SUGGESTED QUESTIONS:**

- How much money have you given Joe? Has he now got 1p more than Sue?
- What other answers are possible?
- What if they each had only one coin? Are all the situations possible?
- How many different answers can you find?

Provide the children with plastic or real coins for them to use for this activity, before they record their answers by drawing the coins.

## Grape fun (page 19)

*Processes: compare, ask own questions*

This activity can help the children to see how many different questions can be asked about a context and encourages them to make up their own questions about the context. Provide the children with red and green pencils.

**SUGGESTED QUESTIONS:**

- How did you work out the answer to this question?
- Did you add the numbers or subtract them?
- How did you know what to do?
- What other questions could you ask?
- How could you answer them?

## Get a grip (page 20)

*Processes: record, reason, be systematic, compare, test ideas*

This activity involves the idea of working systematically in order to find different possibilities. Begin by discussing the coins up to 10p and determine different ways of making amounts up to 10p using those coins. Provide the children with plastic or real coins to help them explore this context and encourage them to record their work using numbers and, if appropriate, the addition sign.

**SUGGESTED QUESTIONS:**

- How many different ways have you found?
- What is the fewest coins that could be held in each hand?
- What are the most coins that could be in one hand?
- How could you record this so that someone else could understand your answers?

## Joke shop sale (page 21)

*Processes: predict, reason, test ideas*

Initially, encourage the children to make predictions about whether there are enough coins to buy each item and then ask them to count to check their predictions. As a further extension activity, invite the children to write their own 'enough' questions for friends to solve.

**SUGGESTED QUESTIONS:**
- How did you find this solution?
- How many more coins are needed?
- How could you write this as a number sentence?

## Pick three cards (page 22)

*Processes: look for pattern, record, reason, make decisions, test ideas, be systematic*

Begin by posing the question 'What totals can be made by adding three numbers between 1 and 5?' This encourages the children to reason about the sizes of the totals first, before testing their ideas practically. Invite them to make their own decisions about how to record their solutions appropriately, and draw attention to those who present their results clearly and in a way that is easily understood. The cards could be laminated to provide a more permanent resource.

**SUGGESTED QUESTIONS:**
- What is the largest/smallest total that can be made with the cards?
- How can you be sure?
- How can you record this for someone else to understand?
- Have you found all the possible solutions?

## Plate, hand, bin (page 23)

*Processes: trial and improvement, look for pattern, record, reason, make decisions, test ideas*

At the start of the lesson, take 6 counters and ask the children how they could share them between a plate, a child's hand, and a bowl. Then ask the children to place the counters so that there is 1 more counter in the bowl than on the plate, and 1 more counter in the child's hand than in the bowl (3 counters in the hand, 2 counters in the bowl and 1 counter on the plate). As the children try to solve these problems, encourage them to talk about what they have tried and the decisions they are making when rearranging the counters. Ensure that they appreciate that both statements must be true for the arrangements of the counters.

**SUGGESTED QUESTIONS:**
- How easy did you find this?
- Did you find the answer straight away?
- What things did you try?
- Can you make up your own puzzles like these for a friend to solve?

## Balloons (page 24)

*Processes: reason, make own decisions, be systematic*

There are only 8 different sets of three numbers with a total of 10 if zero is not included.

| | | | |
|---|---|---|---|
| 1+1+8 | 1+2+7 | 1+3+6 | 1+4+5 |
| 2+2+6 | 2+3+5 | 2+4+4 | |
| 3+3+4 | | | |

Where children have used the same numbers in a different order discuss whether these are related and whether it matters in which order the numbers are added.

**SUGGESTED QUESTIONS:**
- What is similar about these two answers?
- Can you think of a way that uses other numbers?
- How many different ways do you think there are altogether?

## Number clues: 1 and 2 (pages 25–26)

*Processes: reason, look for pattern, ask own questions*

The statements about the secret numbers on page 25 involve odd and even numbers, 'more than' and 'less than' and 'not', such as 'not even', 'not 9'. The statements on page 26 have the same elements plus 'whether the number is a two-digit number', 'closer to one number than another' and 'whether its digits are not the same'. Ensure the children realise that the number must be one of those in the grid and that they should cross off those that the number could not be.

**SOLUTIONS: (1)** 6, 5, 7, 4

**SOLUTIONS: (2)** 13, 6, 14

**SUGGESTED QUESTIONS:**
- How did you work out the secret number?
- Which numbers couldn't it be?
- How do you know?
- Can you think of your own clues for a secret number?

## Glockenspiels (page 27)

*Processes: visualise, look for pattern, record, test ideas, be systematic, generalise*

If possible, demonstrate the differences between notes with a real glockenspiel, counting when a sound (one jump) is made. Ensure that the children understand the meaning of the term 'difference' and watch out for children who interpret this incorrectly as meaning a pair of numbers with 4 other numbers in between, for example they think that 1 and 6 have a difference of 4 as there are four numbers between them. In this instance show difference as jumps on from one number to another. Encourage the children to notice patterns in their answers to the extension activity when compared with the main activity.

**SOLUTIONS:**

1 and 5, 2 and 6, 3 and 7, 4 and 8, 5 and 9, 6 and 10

**NTT**

11 and 15, 12 and 16, 13 and 17, 14 and 18, 15 and 19, 16 and 20

**SUGGESTED QUESTIONS:**
- Have you found all the solutions?
- How can you be sure?
- What if we tried a new difference?
  Would there be more or fewer solutions? Why is that?

## Describe a puzzle or problem using numbers, practical materials and diagrams; use these to solve the problem and set the solution in the original context

The next theme of the Framework's Using and Applying strand deals with Representing. It focuses on children making sense of a problem or puzzle and organising the information in a way that enables them to solve it. In the early years, children may rely on practical materials and diagrams but as they develop confidence in this area may move on to using numbers, calculations and other modelling, including tables, lists or even the use of algebra.

### One each (page 28)

*Processes: estimate, explain, predict, visualise, compare, test ideas*

Children should be encouraged to talk about how they would go about answering the question in the box. Ask them what they would need to do first and then how they would use this to help them answer the question. Focus on the discussion rather than merely completing the activity. Once completed, again discuss strategies used to answer the question and encourage the children to compare their answers.

#### SOLUTIONS:

1 more sharpener, 4 more pencils, 3 more rulers and 2 more erasers.

#### SUGGESTED QUESTIONS:

- Look at this problem. What do you have to find out or do?
- Could you use any resources to help you?
- How did you solve this problem?

### Pete's sweets (page 29)

*Processes: explain, cooperate, look for pattern, record, test ideas, trial and improvement*

The children should be encouraged to talk about how they would go about answering each question. Ask them what they would need to do first and then how they would use this to help them answer the question. Focus on the discussion rather than merely completing the activity. Encourage the children to work together to find different solutions.

#### EXAMPLE SOLUTIONS:

**1** 1p, 4p, 9p, 19p, 49p, 99p, £1.99

**2** 1p (1p is a possible price for the sweets but it is unlikely that a child would have used two 1p coins to pay 1p.) 2p, 5p, 10p, 20p, ...., 3p, 6p, 11p, 21p, ....9p, 14p, 24p... 19p, 29p, 59p .... 39p, 69p...

#### NTT

2p, 3p, 4p, 5p, 6p, 7p, 8p, 10p, 11p, ...

#### SUGGESTED QUESTIONS:

- Look at this problem. What do you have to find out or do?
- Could you use any resources to help you?
- What answers are not possible?
- How do you know?
- How did you solve this problem?

### Bridging (page 30)

*Processes: visualise, look for pattern, record, test ideas, be systematic, generalise, predict*

Allow the children time to make their own observations and decide on their own investigation when using the bridges. It can be useful for the sheet to be copied onto thin card or enlarged to A3 and then laminated to provide a more permanent classroom resource.

Children should notice that the bridge number refers to the difference between the two number being pointed to. Encourage them to begin to predict answers for other bridges not shown, for example bridge 5. Invite the children to predict further solutions if the number line was extended.

#### SUGGESTED QUESTIONS:

- Why do you think the bridges have been numbered in the way they have?
- What answers do you think there might be for a bridge numbered 4, 5 etc.

### How many hatched? (page 31)

*Processes: looking for pattern, recording, explaining, asking own questions, making decisions*

This activity can be used to encourage the children to gain confidence in solving problems using their own method or type of recording. Some children might choose to use apparatus, others might draw the chicks as pictures or as tallies and then count the total. Others might use numbers and standard symbols etc. Discuss the different approaches used at the end of the lesson and draw attention to which recordings can be used to most easily show someone else how to work it out. Encourage children to find out the number of chicks, using whatever method and recording they choose.

#### SOLUTION: 28

#### NOW TRY THIS! 105

#### SUGGESTED QUESTIONS:

- How many chicks hatched on the sixth day?
- How could you work this out?
- What have you drawn? Explain how you worked it out.
- Can you explain to us what you wrote on your sheet?
- How could we explain to someone how many there are?

### Roger's rods (page 32)

*Processes: explain, look for pattern, record, test ideas, trial and improvement*

The children should be encouraged to talk about how they would go about answering each question. Ask them what they would need to do first and then how they would use this to help them answer the question. Focus on the discussion rather than merely completing the activity. Draw attention to those who use numbers rather than pictures to record their answers.

#### SOLUTIONS:

**1** 4 + 2 = 6 (red + green = pink), 6 + 2 = 8 (pink + green = yellow)

**2** 6 − 4 = 2 (pink − red = 2), 8 − 6 = 2 (yellow − pink = 2), 4 − 2 = 2 (red − green = 2)

**3** Half of 6 = 3 (half of pink = blue), half of 8 = 4 (half of yellow = red), half of 4 = 2 (half of red = green)

SUGGESTED QUESTIONS:

- Look at these problems. What do you have to find out or do?
- Could you use any resources to help you?
- How many different solutions have you found?

## Hide the apples (page 33)

*Processes: visualise, make decisions, reason, be systematic, test ideas*

Children will need counters for these activities. Provide them with the sheet and ask them to cover one of the apples with a counter. Initially ask them to say how many apples they can see in each row. Then ask them to see how many they can see in each column, demonstrating the meaning of the word column to the class. Once the children have understood this concept they can attempt the problem-solving activity, trying to place counters in such a way that the number in each row and column is the same.

Draw attention to those children who try a systematic approach and explain that many different solutions are possible.

SUGGESTED QUESTIONS:

- How did you find this solution?
- Have you checked each row and column?
- Is your answer the same as your friend's?
- If you were to do this again, would you try a different way?

## Filling a fish tank (page 34)

*Processes: estimate, explain, reason, record, make own decisions, be systematic*

Again, the children should be encouraged to talk about what they would do to solve this problem. Allow them to make their own decisions about recording and draw attention to those who use numbers and symbols as a way of representing their answers. Collect together all the children's solutions to form a class list of all of them.

SOLUTIONS:

| | |
|---|---|
| 9 cups | 1 + 1 + 1 + 1 + 1 + 1 + 1 + 1 + 1 |
| 6 cups and 1 jug | 1 + 1 + 1 + 1 + 1 + 1 + 3 |
| 4 cups and 1 teapot | 1 + 1 + 1 + 1 + 5 |
| 3 cups and 2 jugs | 1 + 1 + 1 + 3 + 3 |
| 1 teapot, 1 jug and 1 cup | 1 + 3 + 5 |
| 3 jugs | 3 + 3 + 3 |

## Dan's family (page 35)

*Processes: reason, predict, make decisions, trial and improvement*

It is important that children have a chance to think about the possibilities of peoples ages, so begin by discussing how old people in their own families are. As an extension activity, the children could write their own statements about their own family's ages.

POSSIBLE SOLUTIONS:

1 Sisters (if no twins allowed) could be aged 1, 4, 5 or 2, 3, 5 or 1, 2, 7 or 1, 3 6
2 1 and 21, 2 and 22, 3 and 23 etc.
3 1 and 3, 2 and 4, 5 and 6 etc.
4 24 and 48, 25 and 50, 26 and 52, etc.

Assuming that none of the children are the same age they could be aged 1, 2, 5, 6 and 8 or 1, 4, 5, 7 and 9 or 2, 3, 5, 6 and 8 etc.

SUGGESTED QUESTIONS:

- Look at these problems. What do you have to find out or do?
- Could you use any resources to help you?
- How many different solutions have you found?

## Animal magic (page 36)

Processes: reason, record, test ideas, explain, generalise

Children should be encouraged to talk about how they would go about solving the problem. Ask them what they would need to do first and then how they would use this to help them answer the question. Focus on the discussion rather than merely completing the activity. When trying the extension activity, encourage the children to begin to generalise and to notice that the total of the numbers they write in is the number of horses each time.

SOLUTION:

6 horses, 12 animals

SUGGESTED QUESTIONS:

- How could you work this out?
- Why did you decide to record it like this?
- Did you use pictures or another way?

## Answer a question by selecting and using suitable equipment, and sorting information, shapes or objects; display results using tables and pictures

This theme encourages children to pursue lines of enquiry. Initially children learn to ask questions and go on to develop skills of planning, organisation and decision-making. Children need to be taught how to use pictures, lists and diagrams when organising information and supporting their line of enquiry.

## Line dancing (page 37)

*Processes: reason, record, test ideas, explain*

Collect together all the children's solutions to form a class list of all of them.

SOLUTIONS:

| | |
|---|---|
| GGGGGBB | GBGBGGG |
| GGGGBGB | GBGGBGG |
| GGGGBBG | GBGGGBG |
| GGGBBGG | GBGGGGB |
| GGGBGBG | BBGGGGG |
| GGGBGGB | BGBGGGG |
| GGBBGGG | BGGBGGG |
| GGBGBGG | BGGGBGG |
| GGBGGBG | BGGGGBG |
| GGBGGGB | BGGGGGB |
| GBBGGGG | |

SUGGESTED QUESTIONS:

- How many different ways did you find?
- How did you decide how to record your work?

9

## Who sits where? (page 38)

*Processes: be systematic, make decisions, compare, look for pattern, record*

This activity continues with the idea of working systematically, in order to find different possibilities. (There are 24 possibilities.) Initially, the children should work practically with the cards and then be asked to record different solutions. Encourage the children to make their own decisions about how to record the different solutions to this puzzle. Some children might choose to number the children and use numbers to record the different solutions, others may choose to use colours to record the possibilities. Collectively, the different ways found by the whole class could be shown, and the children encouraged to continue to find new ones.

### SUGGESTED QUESTIONS:

- How many different ways could they sit?
- What if this child stayed here and you moved the others?
- Could you find a different way?
- Have you recorded them all?

## Where are the ants? (page 39)

*Processes: reason, visualise, test ideas*

Initially, work together to arrange exactly 15 ants (counters) onto the same arrangement where the number in each line is 8, for example:

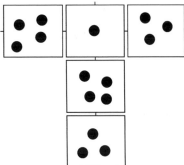

Encourage the children to say which ants could move without changing the totals of each line. Encourage them to try the activity on the sheet and then compare everyone's solutions. Ask the children to say what is similar about everyone's answers (for example: the top middle square of all solutions has 5 ants in).

### SUGGESTED QUESTIONS:

- How many different ways did you find?

## Track tactics (page 40)

*Processes: visualise, trial and improvement, compare*

This activity requires perseverance and some children may not yet be able to visualise a continuous track. Fitting pieces together, however, is very useful in helping children to develop such skills and, even if the child cannot find a 'one track' solution, an arrangement they choose can be stuck down and used for display and discussion. Children who are finding it difficult can be told to put the squares into a 3 x 3 large square and to look for the pieces that might be corner pieces, for example  or the centrepiece

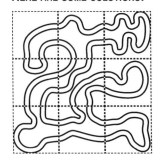 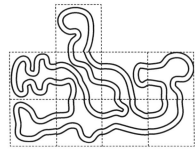

### SUGGESTED QUESTIONS:

- Tell us about your track.
- Did you find this easy/hard? Why do you think that was?

## Spot the leopard (page 41)

*Processes: test ideas, visualise, trial and improvement, be systematic*

In these activities the children must move around the cards showing half leopards so that they create as many leopards as they can with exactly 10 spots. Encourage the children to visualise and try out ideas and draw attention to those who use a systematic approach. Finally, the children could stick the cards onto paper and write the correct numeral under each leopard which can then be displayed.

### SUGGESTED QUESTIONS:

- How many spots on this card?
- Why did you decide to put that there?

## Muddle puzzle (page 42)

*Processes: visualise, look for pattern, compare, make decisions, test ideas*

Children could use the cards to play a game. The cards could be shared between players who then take turns to place a card so that a numeral is correctly made at the side that is joined. As an extension activity, the children could also investigate the highest total possible that could be made by making complete numbers and then adding them together.

### SUGGESTED QUESTIONS:

- Where could you place this card?
- Are there any other positions?

## Toy shop puzzle: 1 and 2 (pages 43–44)

Processes: make decisions, trial and improvement, test ideas, record, explain, reason

If the children need support with their additions, they could place counters or cubes on the 'number boxes' to help them. As an extension activity, the children could record the numbers on the shelves as addition calculations, using the correct sign.

### SOLUTION (1)

1 + 4 , 2 + 3 , 3 + 2 , (in any order or shelf)

### SOLUTION (2)

1 + 2 + 3 , 2 + 4 , 1 + 2 + 3 (in any order or shelf) **or**

3 + 3 , 1 + 1 + 4 , 2 + 2 + 2 (in any order or shelf) **or**

3 + 3 , 2 + 4 , 1 + 1 + 2 + 2 (in any order or shelf)

- How many different ways did you find?
- How could you record this for someone else to follow?

## Fruit trees (page 45)

*Processes: visualise, reason, record, make decisions, test ideas, compare*

Encourage the children to compare their solutions and to think about the maximum and minimum number of pieces of fruit there could be altogether.

### SOLUTIONS:

If 2 in each answer box: 2 x 2 (apples) + 2 x 2 (pears) + 2 (on the ground) = 10.

If 4 in each answer box: 4 x 4 (apples) + 4 x 4 (pears) + 4 (on the ground) = 36.
So answers will be between 10 and 36 inclusive.

### SUGGESTED QUESTION:

- Have you drawn all the apples in the description?

# Describe simple patterns and relationships involving numbers or shapes; decide whether examples satisfy given conditions

> Reasoning should go on in all areas of using and applying mathematics. This theme focuses on making deductions based on patterns, properties and relationships. Children should be encouraged to hear and develop the language and vocabulary of reasoning and to use logical steps when reasoning.

## Letter sorting (page 46)

*Processes: compare, reason, record, make decisions, explain, ask own questions*

Encourage the children to discuss and explain their reasoning and choices and, in particular, to discuss letters that are not clear-cut, for example is there a straight part to the letters y or e? does the dot of the letter i count as a curved line? Ensure that they realise that there are not 'correct' answers to these questions, and that they should make their own decisions and be able to justify them to others

### SUGGESTED QUESTIONS:

- How could you sort these letters?
- Can you explain why you put this letter there?
- How could you record this for others to understand?
- Explain your thinking to a friend.

## Talking shapes (page 47)

*Processes: reason, explain, co-operate, make decisions*

There are no right or wrong ways of sorting these shapes. Some children may collect together those that look similar, whilst others may sort according to straight or curved lines. The importance of this activity is in children being able to explain the features and their reasons for sorting in their particular way. Also, in working with a partner, co-operation skills can be explored. Note that it can be useful to have a spare set of shapes for when the

children become fixed on a shape being in two sets. This can produce valuable discussions. Ask each pair to explain their sorting to the others in the class and discuss differences between the pairs' ideas. If children have stuck the cards on different sheets of paper, these can form a useful display and provoke further discussion.

### SUGGESTED QUESTIONS:

- Can you explain to us about your groups?
- Why did you put this shape here?
- Did anyone else sort theirs in a similar way?

## Dicey dilemmas (page 48)

*Processes: look for pattern, be systematic, cooperate, explain, reason*

For this activity, the children could be given dice or dice cards to help them continue these patterns. Encourage the children to describe any patterns they notice and to talk to a partner, suggesting reasons behind the patterns if they can.

### SUGGESTED QUESTIONS:

- What will be the next dice number in this line?
- Can you tell me about this pattern? What is special about it?

## Domino dilemmas: 1 and 2 (pages 49–50)

*Processes: look for pattern, be systematic, explain, reason*

For this activity, the children could be given dominoes to help them continue these patterns. Encourage the children to describe any patterns they notice and to explain their reasoning.

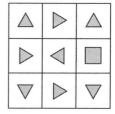

### SUGGESTED QUESTIONS:

- What will be the next domino in this line?
- Can you tell me about this pattern? What is special about it?

## Buckets and spades (page 51)

*Processes: look for pattern, be systematic, explain, reason*

Children can work in pairs or small groups to discuss, recreate and continue these patterns.

### SUGGESTED QUESTIONS:

- What will be the next object in this line?
- Can you tell me about this pattern? What is special about it?

## Odd tile out (page 52)

*Processes: visualise, explain*

This problem-solving activity involves children visualising nine tiles arranged to make a pattern. Some children may find this very difficult whereas others may be quick to spot the odd one out. If any children are having difficulty, copy the sheet onto A3 paper and ask them to cut out the tiles in each pattern and move and rotate them. This will enable them to see similarities and differences more easily.

### SUGGESTED QUESTIONS:

- Which tile is the odd one out?
- How can you be sure?
- What is different about it?

## Even flowers (page 53)

*Processes: look for pattern, reason, predict, generalise, explain, test ideas*

This activity focuses on looking for patterns in the arrangements of even numbers written onto flower beds. Ensure the children understand that they should write the numbers starting at the top left and working from left to right in each row. Encourage the children to describe what they notice to a partner and to use vocabulary such as 'straight lines' and 'diagonal patterns'. Provide a list of even numbers on the board if necessary.

**SUGGESTED QUESTIONS:**

- How many rows has this flower bed?
- How many flowers in each row?
- What patterns do the even numbers form?
- Can you explain your thinking to us? Why do you predict that?
- How good were your predictions?

## Odd, even, odd, even... (page 54)

*Processes: trial and improvement, co-operate, reason, be systematic, explain*

Display a list of odd and even numbers for the children to refer to as they are solving the puzzle. Routes of over 10 numbers are possible but it is not possible to find a route that uses all the numbers as there are sections where there are too many evens, or too many odds close together.

**EXAMPLE SOLUTIONS:**

5, 12, 5 (3 numbers); 4, 7, 8, 5, 2, 1, 6, 9, 16 (9 numbers); 1, 2, 5, 12, 3, 8, 7, 8, 5, 4, 9, 6, 5, 10  (14 numbers)

**SUGGESTED QUESTIONS:**

- How long is your route?
- Can you find a longer one?

## Flower power (page 55)

*Processes: reason, compare, explain*

As an extension activity, the children could make up their own similar puzzles for a partner to tackle.

**SOLUTIONS:**

no colours 1, 7, 11, 13, 17, 19

1 colour 2, 3, 5, 9, 14,

2 colours 4, 8, 10, 15, 16,

3 colours 6, 18, 20

4 colours 12

**SUGGESTED QUESTIONS:**

- Can you see any patterns in the numbers?
- What do you think is special about the number 12?

## Ladybird party (page 56)

*Processes: visualise, predict, estimate, test ideas*

This activity provides practice in the important skill of visualising sets of numbers in smaller groups, rather than needing to count items individually. After the children have completed the activity and compared their predictions with the actual numbers of dots, discuss ways of seeing objects in groups of threes or fours. Ask which shapes they found it easy to get an idea of the number without counting, for example 'I saw two patterns of 5s like on a dice in this shape so I knew there were 10 dots.' Dots could be masked and a greater/fewer number drawn to provide a flexible resource for children of different abilities.

**SUGGESTED QUESTIONS:**

- What did you see in your mind when you tried to guess which shapes had 7/8/9 dots in them?
- How good were your predictions?
- Could you count these by grouping in threes or fours?

# Describe ways of solving puzzles and problems, explaining choices and decisions orally or using pictures

The final theme is Communicating, including both oral and recorded communications. Children should be given opportunities to express their thinking, their reasoning and to communicate their findings to others and also to make personal records of their own. In lessons, the children should be encouraged to work with others, discussing decisions to be made, describing actions taken and conclusions made.

## Lots or few? (page 57)

*Processes: make decisions, record, co-operate, estimate, compare*

The focus of this activity is on children making decisions as to whether there are only a few items or a lot of items around the school. Children should work in pairs and discuss things around the classroom and school and agree on items to record in each column. Given the non-exact nature of the terms 'a lot' and 'a few' the children may disagree about certain items. 'Are there a lot of light-switches in the school or a few?' Encourage them to appreciate that there are no right or wrong answers, only the children's opinions. Once they have made estimates of the number of 'a few' items, invite the children, as a class, to come to a consensus and generalise about how many we usually mean when we say 'a few', for example more than 1 and less than 10.

**SUGGESTED QUESTIONS:**

- Which things are there a lot of/a few of?
- How did you record this?
- Did you always agree? Which did you disagree on?
- How many of each thing in 'a few of' group were there?
- What does this tell us about what we mean by a few?

## Share the cheese (page 58)

*Processes: make decisions, test ideas, trial and improvement, reason*

Children should be encouraged to talk about how they would go about solving the problem. Ensure that they understand the two statements and appreciate that both statements must be true for the solution. Ask them what they would need to do first and then how they would use this to help them answer the question.

**EXAMPLE SOLUTION:**

Cut the cheese into 12 pieces. Give Mummy mouse 4 pieces and Mini mouse 2 pieces. Molly and Milly get 3 pieces each, making 12 altogether.

Other solutions could be found if the block was cut into other numbers of pieces.

**SUGGESTED QUESTIONS:**

- What would you do to help the mouse family?
- How would you try to solve this problem?

## Maths Challenge (page 59)

*Processes: record, make decisions, compare, estimate, ask own questions*

The children should work in groups and agree on a task. They should discuss and agree on how this task can be carried out, deciding on rules and how scores might be given, for example 3 points for winning, 2 for coming second and 1 for third. Each child should record the results on a recording sheet. Stress the importance of showing information clearly, as an aid to memory and for others to use. More than one task can be carried out and an overall winner found, using the scoring system agreed.

**SUGGESTED QUESTIONS:**

- How could we score each round?
- How could we find out which person is in the lead at the moment?

## Doodlepots (page 60)

*Processes: compare, visualise, look for pattern, be systematic*

Once the children have decorated their pots a display can be organised in a structured way, for example all the pots with spots and stripes could be shown together. This can help the children to begin to think systematically.

**SUGGESTED QUESTIONS:**

- How many pots have stripes?
- Is there another pattern you could use instead?

## Ed the explorer (page 61)

*Processes: test ideas, visualise, trial and improvement, be systematic*

In this activity the children must move Ed the explorer around and put him in different positions on the grid. They should be encouraged to notice that sometimes he is touching others (and/or rabbits and elephants) and sometimes he is not. They should then try to find specific positions to match the given rules. Encourage children to visualise and try out ideas and draw attention to those who use a systematic approach. Point out that there can sometimes be more than one solution. Finally, the children could stick Ed onto their sheet in a particular position and these could be displayed, describing how many bears (and/or rabbits and elephants) he is touching each time.

**SUGGESTED QUESTIONS:**

- Can you see any positions where you think he will touch 1 bear? 2 bears? 3 bears?
- Put him there now. Were you correct?
- Are there any other places you could put him that would mean he was touching the same number of bears?
- Who is Ed touching in this position?

## Balancing act (page 62)

*Processes: reason, test ideas, visualise, predict, look for pattern*

**SOLUTIONS:**

Sheep and Badger 1 cube each

Egg monster 2 cubes

Lion 3 cubes

Piglet 4 cubes

So piglet is heaviest and the badger and sheep weigh the same.

**NTT** 5 cubes

**SUGGESTED QUESTIONS:**

- How heavy is the lion?
- How can you describe that?
- Is the lion heavier than the piglet?
- Is the badger lighter than the sheep?

## Ben's pets (page 63)

*Processes: reason, compare, explain, ask own questions*

Children should be encouraged to talk about how they would go about solving the problems. Ask them what they would need to do first and then how they would use this to help them answer the question. Focus on the discussion rather than merely completing the activity.

**SOLUTIONS:**

| | |
|---|---|
| add | subtract |
| add | add |
| subtract | subtract |

**SUGGESTED QUESTIONS:**

- How would you work out the answer?
- Would you add or subtract?
- What clues might the words 'altogether' or 'left' give you?

## Flo's florists (page 64)

*Processes: reason, compare, explain, ask own questions*

As for the previous activity, the children should be encouraged to talk about how they would go about solving the problems.

**SOLUTIONS:**

| | |
|---|---|
| add | subtract |
| subtract | add |
| subtract | add |

**SUGGESTED QUESTIONS:**

- How would you work out the answer?
- Would you add or subtract?

# Using the CD-ROM

The PC CD-ROM included with this book contains an easy-to-use software program that allows you to print out pages from the book, to view them (e.g. on an interactive whiteboard) or to customise the activities to suit the needs of your pupils.

## Getting started

It's easy to run the software. Simply insert the CD-ROM into your CD drive and the disk should autorun and launch the interface in your web browser.

If the disk does not autorun, open 'My Computer' and select the CD drive, then open the file 'start.html'.

Please note: this CD-ROM is designed for use on a PC. It will also run on most Apple Macintosh computers in Safari however, due to the differences between Mac and PC fonts, you may experience some unavoidable variations in the typography and page layouts of the activity sheets.

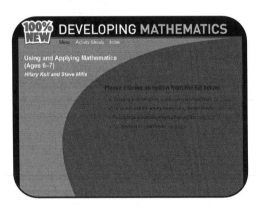

## The Menu screen

Four options are available to you from the main menu screen.

The first option takes you to the Activity Sheets screen, where you can choose an activity sheet to edit or print out using Microsoft Word.

(If you do not have the Microsoft Office suite, you might like to consider using OpenOffice instead. This is a multi-platform and multi-lingual office suite, and an 'open-source' project. It is compatible with all other major office suites, and the product is free to download, use and distribute. The homepage for OpenOffice on the Internet is: www.openoffice.org.)

The second option on the main menu screen opens a PDF file of the entire book using Adobe Reader (see below). This format is ideal for printing out copies of the activity sheets or for displaying them, for example on an interactive whiteboard.

The third option allows you to choose a page to edit from a text-only list of the activity sheets, as an alternative to the graphical interface on the Activity Sheets screen.

Adobe Reader is free to download and to use. If it is not already installed on your computer, the fourth link takes you to the download page on the Adobe website.

You can also navigate directly to any of the three screens at any time by using the tabs at the top.

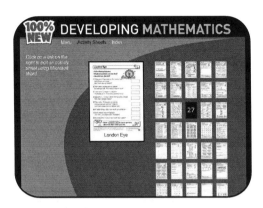

## The Activity Sheets screen

This screen shows thumbnails of all the activity sheets in the book. Rolling the mouse over a thumbnail highlights the page number and also brings up a preview image of the page.

Click on the thumbnail to open a version of the page in Microsoft Word (or an equivalent software program, see above.) The full range of editing tools are available to you here to customise the page to suit the needs of your particular pupils. You can print out copies of the page or save a copy of your edited version onto your computer.

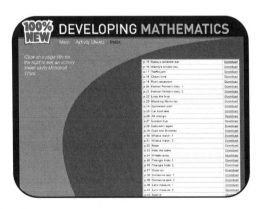

## The Index screen

This is a text-only version of the Activity Sheets screen described above. Choose an activity sheet and click on the 'download' link to open a version of the page in Microsoft Word to edit or print out.

## Technical support

If you have any questions regarding the *100% New Developing Literacy* or *Developing Mathematics* software, please email us at the address below. We will get back to you as quickly as possible.

educationalsales@acblack.com

# Penguins

- **Write numbers between** 1 **and** 5 **in the boxes.**
- **Choose penguins to colour from the ice-floes.**

- **I will colour** ☐ **penguins.**

- **I will colour** ☐ **penguins.**

- **I will colour** ☐ **penguins.**

- **I will colour** ☐ **penguins.**

- **Tell a friend how many penguins have not been coloured.**

**Teachers' note** Remind the children that they must only colour the number of penguins they have written in each box and that they can be from either ice-floe in each pair. When recording their solutions, encourage the children to make their own choices about how to do this. Some may choose to use words or signs, others may use addition/subtraction. Talk together about their recordings.

**100% New Developing Mathematics
Using and Applying Mathematics:
Ages 5–6**
**© A & C BLACK**

# Flapjacks

- **Cut out the flapjacks. Put them in order of** $\boxed{\text{length}}$ .
- **Pick the flapjack with a bite taken out.**
  **Find all the cards that are** $\boxed{\text{shorter}}$ **than it.**
  **Find all the cards that are** $\boxed{\text{longer}}$ **than it.**

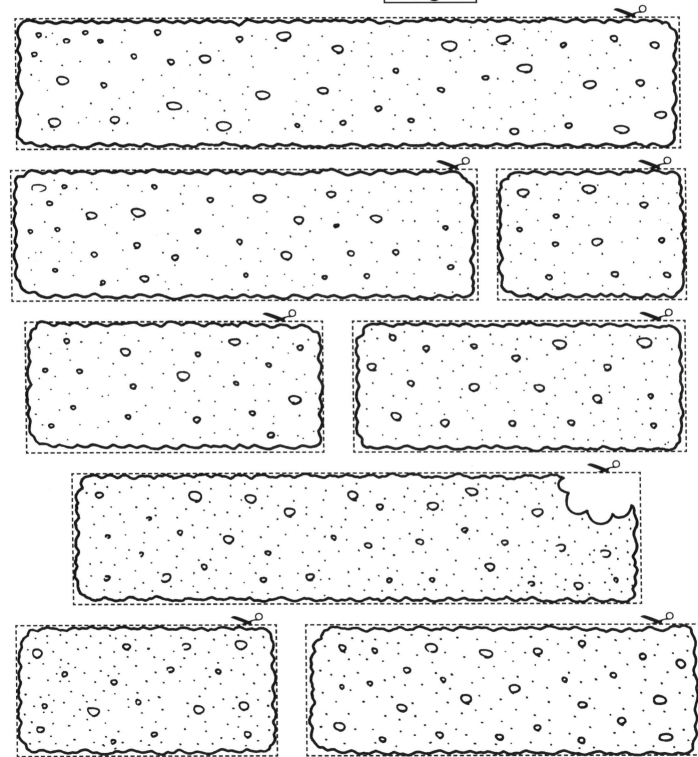

**Teachers' note** Ask questions to encourage the children to think about the lengths of the flapjacks and to sort and organise them in different ways. Use appropriate vocabulary such as longer, shorter, longest, shortest, half as long, twice as long, etc.

**100% New Developing Mathema**
**Using and Applying Mathematic**
**Ages 5–6**
**© A & C BLACK**

- **Count the shoes.**
- **How many** pairs **?**
- **How many** odd ones **?**

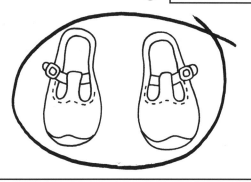

| 3 | shoes |
| 1 | pairs |
| 1 | odd ones |

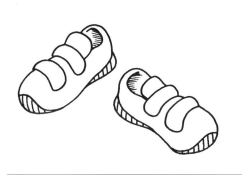

| | shoes |
| | pairs |
| | odd ones |

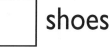

| | shoes |
| | pairs |
| | odd ones |

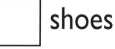

| | shoes |
| | pairs |
| | odd ones |

**Teachers' note** Ask the children to draw a loop around each pair of shoes. Encourage them to look for patterns in the numbers and discuss odd and even numbers. As an extension activity, ask the children to draw 11 shoes on the back of the sheet. How many pairs/odd ones? Repeat the activity for 13 shoes.

**100% New Developing Mathematics Using and Applying Mathematics: Ages 5–6**
© A & C BLACK

# Money, money

- **How much money might be in each purse?**
- **Draw the coins. Write how much.**
- **Joe has 1 penny more than Sue.**

Joe

Sue

- **Ben has 2 pence more than Li.**

Ben

Li

- **Urvi has 3 pence more than Dan.**

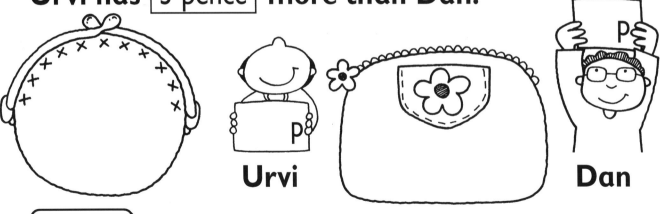

Urvi

Dan

**NOW TRY THIS!**

- **Draw other amounts of money that Urvi and Dan could have.**

**Teachers' note** Ensure the children realise that many answers are possible. Encourage them to choose amounts different from their friends and then discuss the different answers. Talk about strategies used, such as drawing the same coins in each purse first and then drawing the extra amount in the first purse.

**100% New Developing Mathemat**
**Using and Applying Mathematics**
**Ages 5–6**
**© A & C BLACK**

**18**

# Grape fun

- Colour $\boxed{4}$ grapes red and $\boxed{3}$ grapes green.

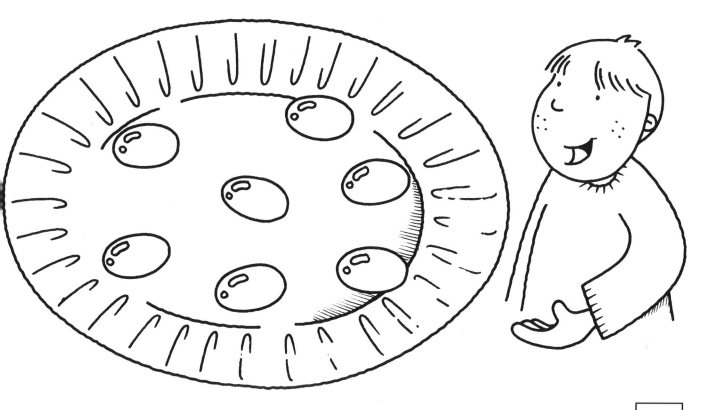

- How many more grapes are red than green? ☐

- How many grapes are there $\boxed{\text{altogether}}$? ☐

- How many more grapes are needed to have $\boxed{10}$? ☐

- I eat $\boxed{1}$ green grape. How many grapes are left? ☐

- I also eat $\boxed{3}$ red ones. How many grapes are left now? ☐

**NOW TRY THIS!**

- Make up some more grape questions of your own for a friend to answer.

**Teachers' note** This sheet and grape context can provide a wide range of opportunities for the children to solve problems and make up and answer their own questions. Encourage them to explain how they worked out each answer and to describe strategies used. Provide the children with red and green pencils.

**100% New Developing Mathematics Using and Applying Mathematics: Ages 5–6**
© A & C BLACK

**19**

# Get a grip

- **There is a total of** $\boxed{11\text{p}}$ **being held in these hands.**

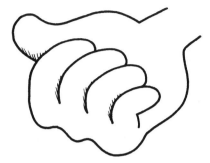 

- **What coins could be in each hand?**
- **Show some different ways below.**

**Teachers' note** As an extension activity, ask the children to show more ways on another piece of paper. How many different ways might there be? Encourage them to discuss the possibilities, including whether it is acceptable for there to be no coins in one hand. Draw attention to any systematic recording. The amount could be changed to provide variation and differentiation.

**100% New Developing Mathemati**
**Using and Applying Mathematics**
**Ages 5–6**
© A & C BLACK

# Joke shop sale

- **Is there enough money to buy each item?**
- **Write** yes **or** no.

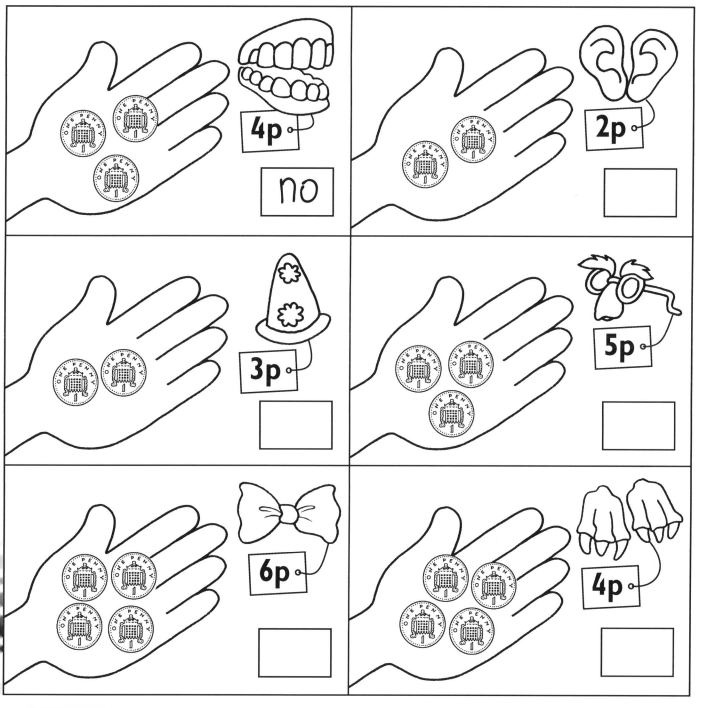

|  |  |
|---|---|
| 4p — **no** | 2p — |
| 3p — | 5p — |
| 6p — | 4p — |

**NOW TRY THIS!**

- **If there is not enough money,** draw **the extra coins you need in the hand.**

**Teachers' note** Discuss the term 'enough' and ensure that children understand its meaning. Children could be provided with coins and asked to show the correct amount for each item with real or plastic coins.

**100% New Developing Mathematics Using and Applying Mathematics: Ages 5–6**
© A & C BLACK

21

# Pick three cards

- Cut out the cards. Pick ⬚3⬚ cards.
- What totals can be made?

| 1 | 1 | 1 | 1 |
|---|---|---|---|
| 2 | 2 | 2 | 3 |
| 3 | 3 | 4 | 4 |
| 4 | 5 | 5 | 5 |

# Plate, hand, bin

- **You need** exactly **10 counters.**
- **Arrange the counters to solve each problem.**

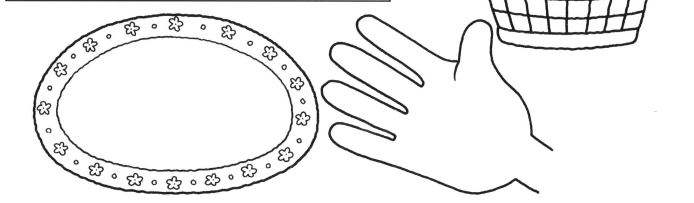

- **Put** 3 more **counters on the plate than the hand.**
- **Put** 1 more **counter in the bin than on the hand.**

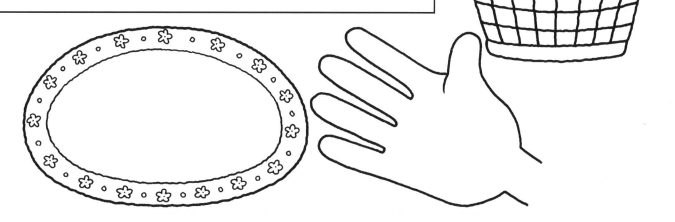

- **Put** twice **as many counters on the plate as on the hand.**
- **Put** 2 **more counters in the bin than on the hand.**

**Teachers' note** Ensure the children understand that all 10 counters must be used for each problem and that both statements must be taken into account when arranging them. As an extension activity, the children could make up their own plate, hand, bin puzzles.

**100% New Developing Mathematics
Using and Applying Mathematics:
Ages 5–6**
© A & C BLACK

**23**

# Balloons

- **Write a number on each balloon.**
- **Each child's balloons must add up to** 10 .

4  5  1

---

**Teachers' note** Alter the numbers before printing /copying to create differentiated activities. Discuss whether it matters in which order the children add the numbers.

**100% New Developing Mathema**
**Using and Applying Mathematics**
**Ages 5–6**
**© A & C BLACK**

Here are the clues to some secret numbers.
- **Cross off the numbers they cannot be .**
  **What are the numbers?**

| 1 | 2 | 3 | 4 | 5 |
|---|---|---|---|---|
| 6 | 7 | 8 | 9 | 10 |

It is more than 4.
It is even.
It is less than 7.

| 1 | 2 | 3 | 4 | 5 |
|---|---|---|---|---|
| 6 | 7 | 8 | 9 | 10 |

It is more than 3.
It is odd.
It is less than 7.

| 1 | 2 | 3 | 4 | 5 |
|---|---|---|---|---|
| 6 | 7 | 8 | 9 | 10 |

It is more than 5.
It is not even.
It is not 9.

| 1 | 2 | 3 | 4 | 5 |
|---|---|---|---|---|
| 6 | 7 | 8 | 9 | 10 |

It is more than 2.
It is not odd.
It is less than 6.

**NOW TRY THIS!**

- **Choose a secret number. Make up your own clues.**

| 1 | 2 | 3 | 4 | 5 |
|---|---|---|---|---|
| 6 | 7 | 8 | 9 | 10 |

_____

_____

_____

**Teachers' note** Demonstrate how, as each clue is read, the numbers that the secret number could not be are crossed off, for example if it is more than 4, the numbers 1, 2, 3, 4 should be crossed off.

100% New Developing Mathematics
Using and Applying Mathematics:
Ages 5–6
© A & C BLACK

**25**

Here are the clues to some secret numbers.

• **Cross off the numbers that the secret numbers cannot be. What are the numbers?**

| 1 | 2 | 3 | 4 | 5 |
|---|---|---|---|---|
| 6 | 7 | 8 | 9 | 10 |
| 11 | 12 | 13 | 14 | 15 |

It is more than 9.
It is odd.
It is less than 15.
Its digits are not the same.

| 1 | 2 | 3 | 4 | 5 |
|---|---|---|---|---|
| 6 | 7 | 8 | 9 | 10 |
| 11 | 12 | 13 | 14 | 15 |

It is less than 8.
It is even.
It is written without any straight lines.

| 1 | 2 | 3 | 4 | 5 |
|---|---|---|---|---|
| 6 | 7 | 8 | 9 | 10 |
| 11 | 12 | 13 | 14 | 15 |

It is a 2-digit number
It is even.
It is closer to 15 than to 10.

---

**NOW TRY THIS!**

• **Choose a secret number. Make up your own clues.**

| 1 | 2 | 3 | 4 | 5 |
|---|---|---|---|---|
| 6 | 7 | 8 | 9 | 10 |
| 11 | 12 | 13 | 14 | 15 |

_____

_____

_____

---

**Teachers' note** Demonstrate how, as each clue is read, the numbers that the secret number could not be are crossed off, for example if it is more than 4, the numbers 1, 2, 3, 4 should be crossed off.

**100% New Developing Mathemat**
**Using and Applying Mathematics**
**Ages 5–6**
**© A & C BLACK**

# Glockenspiels

**Ruby plays** two **notes.**

**The** difference **between them is 4.**

| 1 | 2 | 3 | 4 | 5 | 6 | 7 | 8 | 9 | 10 |

**Which** two **notes might Ruby have played?**

• **Record your work here.**

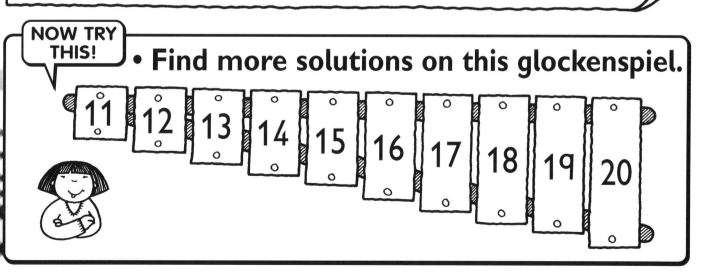

**NOW TRY THIS!**

• **Find more solutions on this glockenspiel.**

| 11 | 12 | 13 | 14 | 15 | 16 | 17 | 18 | 19 | 20 |

**Teachers' note** The difference can be changed before printing/copying to provide differentiation and variety. Draw attention to systematic work and encourage the children to be sure that they have found all the possible solutions each time.

**100% New Developing Mathematics
Using and Applying Mathematics:**
*Ages 5–6*
© A & C BLACK

**27**

• **How can you find out the answer to this question?**

How many more are needed so that every child has one each?

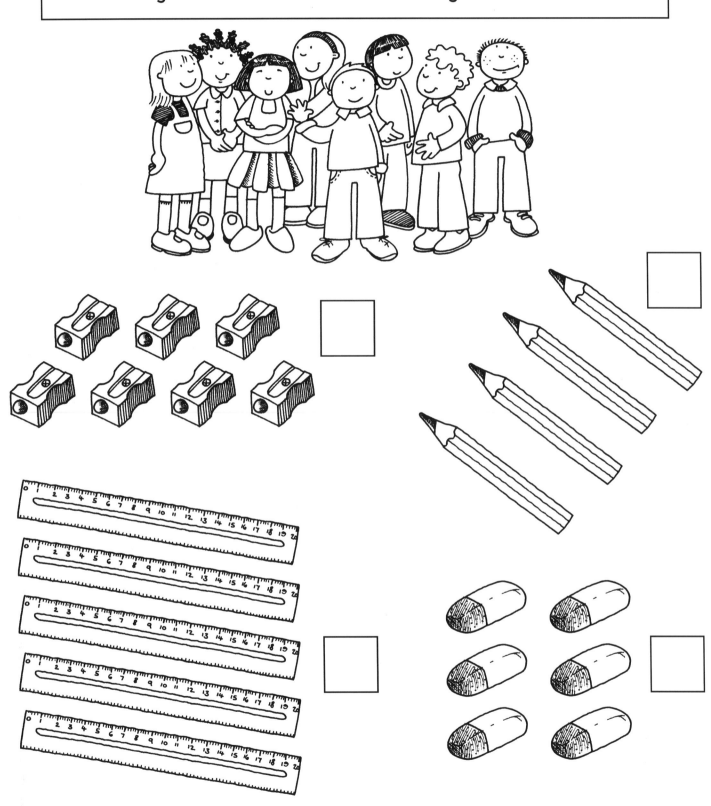

**Teachers' note** Encourage the children to explain how they think these problems could be solved and to use numbers to represent the problems. As an extension activity, the children could represent each problem as a number sentence where the answer is the solution, for example: 8 – 5 = 3. Some items could be masked before copying to include variety.

**100% New Developing Mathemat**
**Using and Applying Mathematics**
**Ages 5–6**
© A & C BLACK

# Pete's sweets

• **Work with a friend to find as many answers as you can.**

**Pete buys some sweets.**

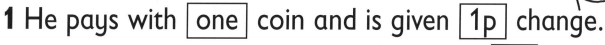

**1** He pays with |one| coin and is given |1p| change.

How much could the sweets have cost? ☐

**2** He pays with |two| coins and is given |1p| change.

How much could the sweets have cost? ☐

**NOW TRY THIS!**

**Pete buys some sweets with |three| coins and is given |1p| change.**

**• How much could the sweets have cost?** ☐

**Teachers' note** Encourage the children to set the rules for this investigation, such as deciding whether Pete is allowed to have two coins that are same or whether the coins must be silver coins. These constraints could be suggested to create variation. Ensure that children work systematically and take into account all coins in circulation. Draw attention to good methods of recording.

**100% New Developing Mathematics**
**Using and Applying Mathematics:**
**Ages 5–6**
**© A & C BLACK**

**29**

# Bridging

- ## Cut out the bridges below.
- ## Choose a bridge and place it above the number line so that the arrows point to numbers.
- ## Record the numbers. Try the bridge in different places.

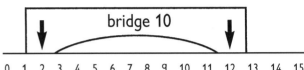

0 1 2 3 4 5 6 7 8 9 10 11 12 13 14 15

## 0 1 2 3 4 5 6 7 8 9 10 11 12 13 14 15

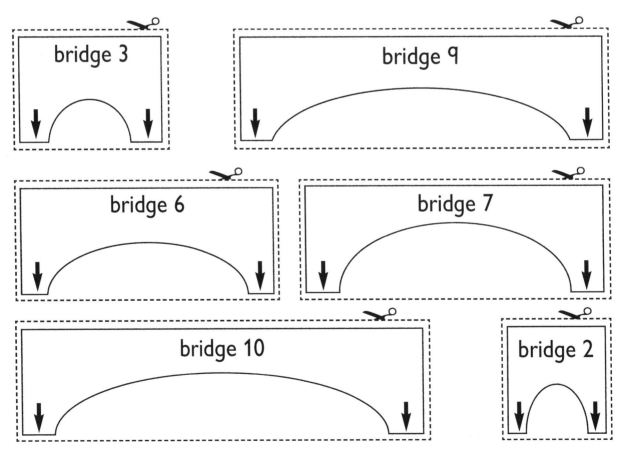

bridge 3

bridge 9

bridge 6

bridge 7

bridge 10

bridge 2

**Teachers' note** Provide the children with paper on which to record their findings. Encourage the children to explore as many different possible solutions as they can and to record them in a suitable way. Discuss why the bridges are numbered in the way they are and encourage the children to describe their solutions using number sentences for addition or subtraction.

**100% New Developing Mathema**
**Using and Applying Mathematic**
**Ages 5–6**
**© A & C BLACK**

# How many hatched?

- **Talk to a friend about how you can solve this problem.**

On **Day 1**, Monday, ☐1☐ chick hatched.

On **Day 2**, Tuesday, ☐2☐ chicks hatched.

On **Day 3**, Wednesday, ☐3☐ chicks hatched.

On **Day 4**, Thursday, ☐4☐ chicks hatched,

and so on…. until

on **Day 7**, Sunday, ☐7☐ chicks hatched.

- **How many chicks hatched altogether in this week?** ☐

- **Record** your work here.

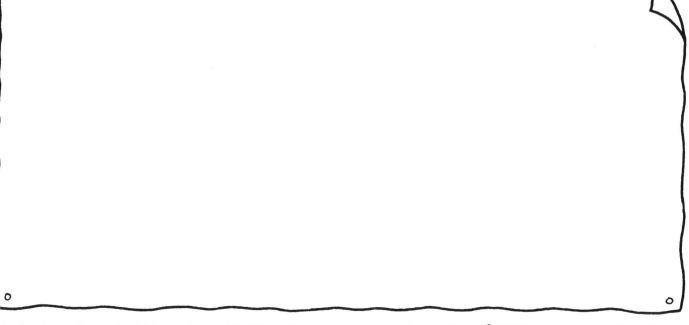

**Teachers' note** Ensure the children understand that the pattern continues for days 5, 6 and 7 etc. As an extension activity, ask the children to work out how many chicks would hatch altogether in 2 weeks if the pattern continued for days 8 to 14. Encourage the children to make their own decisions about method and recording.

**100% New Developing Mathematics Using and Applying Mathematics: Ages 5–6** © A & C BLACK

# Roger's rods

Roger joins cubes in a line to make rods.
• Shade the rods in the colours shown.

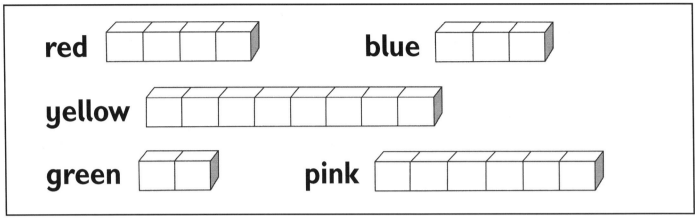

red

blue

yellow

green

pink

**1** Which ⌜two⌝ rods together are the same length as another rod?

_____

**2** Which ⌜two⌝ rods have a difference of ⌜2⌝ cubes?

_____

**3** Which rod is ⌜half⌝ the length of another?

_____

NOW TRY THIS!

**Roger made another rod using ⌜7⌝ white cubes.**

• **Are there now more answers to the questions?**

Teachers' note Some children might benefit from making the rods out of coloured cubes.
Encourage the children to make their own decisions about how to record the solutions and to
consider whether there is more than one solution to each problem.

100% New Developing Mathemat
Using and Applying Mathematics
Ages 5–6
© A & C BLACK

# Hide the apples

- **Put counters on the apples to hide them, so that you can only see** 2 **apples in each row and column.**

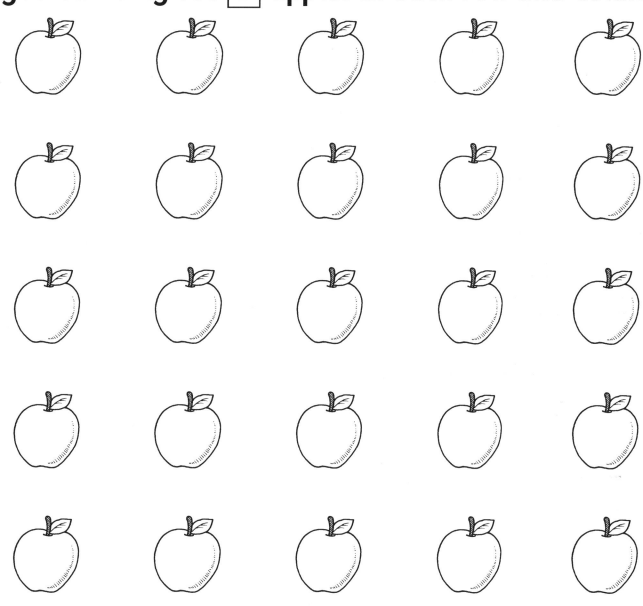

**NOW TRY THIS!**

- **Add** 1 more **row of apples. Make up your own puzzle.**

**Teachers' note** It is vital that children understand what is meant by row and column for this activity. Provide them couith counters and explain that they can cover any of the apples, but you must be able to still see 2 apples in each row, going across, and 2 apples in each column, going down. Explain that there are many different possible solutions.

100% New Developing Mathematics
Using and Applying Mathematics:
Ages 5–6
© A & C BLACK

**33**

# Filling a fish tank

**1 cup of water**   **3 cups of water**   **5 cups of water**

This tank needs ⑨ cups of water.
Which containers could you use?
- Find different ways you could do this.
- Show your work here.

- **What if the fish tank needed 10 cups of water?**

**Teachers' note** Encourage the children to find as many different solutions as they can. Before copying, change the number of cupfuls needed, to create a wide range of questions for children to solve. When recording, the children may choose to draw the containers but draw attention to any children who begin to use numbers to help them represent this problem.

**100% New Developing Mathemat**
**Using and Applying Mathematics**
**Ages 5–6**
**© A & C BLACK**

# Dan's family

• **Meet Dan's family.**

---

**1** Dan has three sisters. Their ages add up to 10. How old could they be?

---

**2** Dan's dad is 20 years older than Dan. How old could Dan and his dad be?

---

**3** Dan has one brother. Dan is 2 years younger than him. How old could Dan and his brother be?

---

**4** Dan's mum is half the age of his gran. How old could they both be?

---

**Teachers' note** Encourage the children to discuss their thoughts and reasoning with a friend and stress that there is not enough information to be sure of the ages at this stage. At the end of the activity, the children could suggest the most likely ages for Dan's family.

**100% New Developing Mathematics**
**Using and Applying Mathematics:**
**Ages 5–6**
**© A & C BLACK**

# Animal magic

In a field ⬚half⬚ the animals are horses.
There are also ⬚2⬚ cows, ⬚1⬚ sheep
and ⬚3⬚ pigs.

• **How many horses are there?** _____

• **How many animals are there?** _____

**NOW TRY THIS!**

• **Write some** ⬚different⬚ **numbers in the boxes and solve the new problem.
In a field** ⬚half⬚ **the animals are horses.
There are also** ⬚ ⬚ **cows,** ⬚ ⬚ **sheep
and** ⬚ ⬚ **pigs.**

• **How many horses are there?** _____

• **How many animals are there?** _____

**Teachers' note** Introduce the activity by saying that a farmer needs to know how many animals are in the field so he can plan to build them a new field. Encourage the children to create a range of new questions of this type and to explain how each question could be solved. More confident children could explore solutions when one quarter of the animals are horses.

100% New Developing Mathema
Using and Applying Mathematics
Ages 5–6
© A & C BLACK

# Line dancing

• **Cut out the cards to help you solve the problem.**

5 girls stand in a line.

2 boys join them.

How many different ways can they line up?

• **Use the space below to record your answers.**

**Teachers' note** Encourage the children to make their own decisions about how to record the solutions, such as perhaps using the letters G and B to stand for girls and boys. Invite the children to collaborate in order to find new solutions and come to a general agreement about how many different solutions there are altogether.

**100% New Developing Mathematics**
**Using and Applying Mathematics:**
**Ages 5–6**
**© A & C BLACK**

# Who sits where?

- **Cut out the children below.**
- **How many different ways can you put the children in the chairs?**

- **Record your answers here.**

**Teachers' note** Encourage the children to make their own decisions about how to record the different solutions to this puzzle. Some children might choose to number the children and use numbers to record the different solutions. For variation, one child and one chair could be removed before copying to create an easier challenge.

**38**

**100% New Developing Mathematic**
**Using and Applying Mathematics**
**Ages 5–6**
**© A & C BLACK**

# Where are the ants?

- **Arrange the 15 counters on the paving slabs so that there are** $\boxed{10}$ **in each line.**

You need
15 counters to
stand for ants

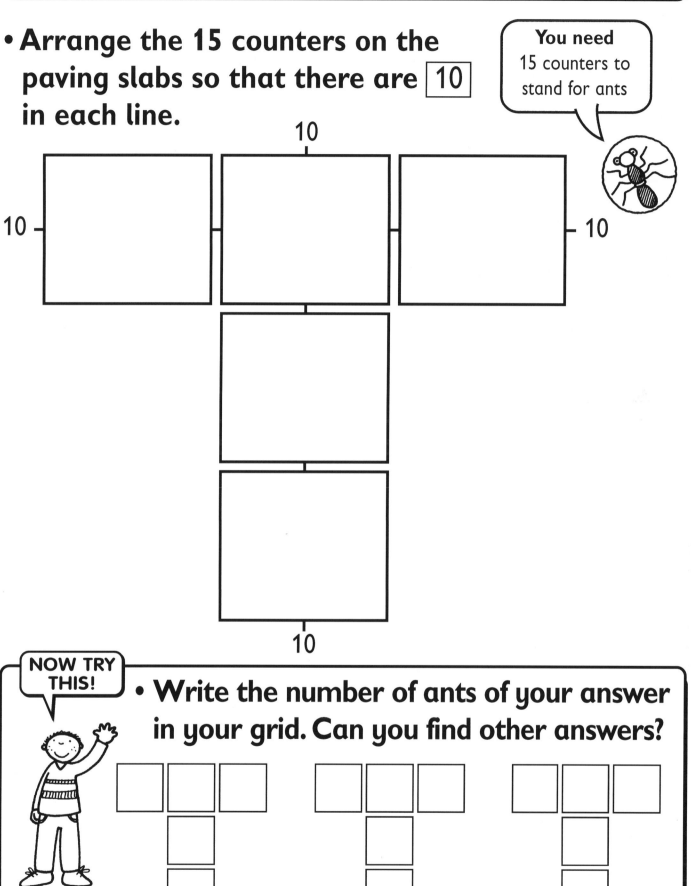

**NOW TRY THIS!**

- **Write the number of ants of your answer in your grid. Can you find other answers?**

Teachers' note The number in each line can be changed before copying to create variety, for example to 8, 9 or 11. Encourage the children to explain how they tackled the problem and to use numbers to record their solutions.

100% New Developing Mathematics
Using and Applying Mathematics:
Ages 5–6
© A & C BLACK

# Track tactics

- **Cut out the squares.**
- **Arrange them to make** $\boxed{1}$ **continuous track.**

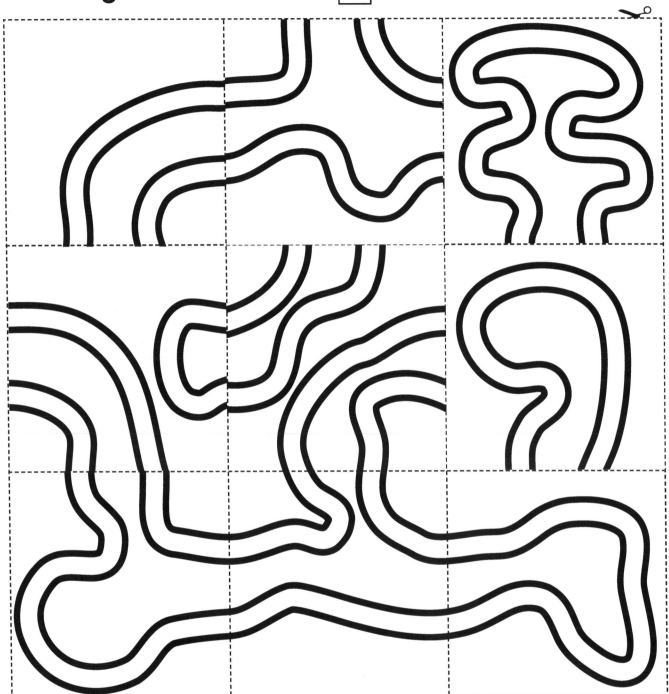

**NOW TRY THIS!**

- **How can you arrange the cards to make more than** $\boxed{1}$ **continuous track?**

**Teachers' note** This sheet could be enlarged onto A3 paper or copied onto card and laminated for a more permanent resource. See page 10 for more information on this game.

**100% New Developing Mathemat**
**Using and Applying Mathematics**
**Ages 5–6**
© A & C BLACK

# Spot the leopard

• **Cut out the cards. Can all the cards be used to make leopards with** 10 **spots?**

**Teachers' note** The number in the box can be changed to any number between 8 and 12 before copying. Not all leopard pieces might be used but children can explore which total between 8 and 12 can use all the pieces.

**100% New Developing Mathematics Using and Applying Mathematics:** Ages 5–6 © A & C BLACK

**41**

# Muddle puzzle

- **Cut out the cards.**
- **Join them to make the numbers 1 to 4.**
- **Can you arrange the cards in different ways?**

Teachers' note Children use the cards to play a game. The cards are shared between two players who take turns to place a card so that a numeral is correctly made at the side that is joined.

100% New Developing Mathematics
Using and Applying Mathematics:
Ages 5–6
© A & C BLACK

The number on the box shows how many cars are inside.

- Cut out the boxes below.
- Arrange them so that there are 5 cars on each shelf.

**Teachers' note** Encourage the children to find different ways to complete this puzzle. The following sheet can be used to provide a further challenge, Some children might find it useful to draw the cars as dots on the boxes and then to use the dots to help them.

**100% New Developing Mathematics**
**Using and Applying Mathematics:**
**Ages 5–6**
**© A & C BLACK**

The number on the box shows how many cars are inside.

- Cut out the boxes below.
- Arrange them so that there are $\boxed{6}$ cars on each shelf.

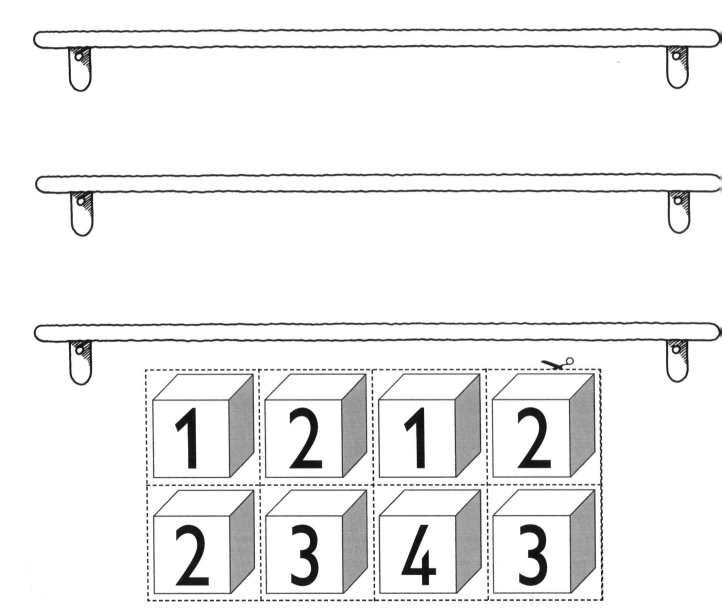

**Teachers' note** Encourage the children to find different solutions to this puzzle and to record them on paper. Discuss suitable ways of recording and ask children to collaborate to find further solutions. The previous sheet can be used to introduce the activity.

**100% New Developing Mathemat**
**Using and Applying Mathematics**
**Ages 5–6**
**© A & C BLACK**

# Fruit trees

• **Write the number** $\boxed{2}$, $\boxed{3}$ **or** $\boxed{4}$ **in the boxes below.**

In the garden there are $\boxed{\phantom{0}}$ apple trees
and $\boxed{\phantom{0}}$ pear trees.
On each apple tree there are $\boxed{\phantom{0}}$ apples.
On each pear tree there are $\boxed{\phantom{0}}$ pears.
There are $\boxed{\phantom{0}}$ fallen apples on the ground.

• **Where are the apples and pears in the garden?**
**Draw a picture of the garden.**

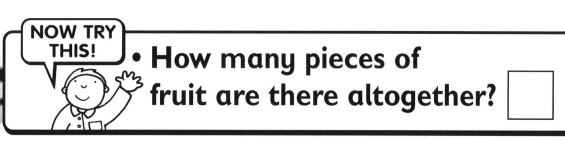

**NOW TRY THIS!**

• **How many pieces of fruit are there altogether?** $\boxed{\phantom{0}}$

---

**Teachers' note** Ensure the children appreciate that each garden will be different according to the numbers written into the boxes. Encourage them to compare their solutions and to think about the maximum number of pieces of fruit there could be altogether.

**100% New Developing Mathematics**
**Using and Applying Mathematics:**
**Ages 5–6**
© A & C BLACK

# Letter sorting

Are letters written using straight or curved lines?

- **Write these letters in the correct columns of the table.**

# c l o v b x p h k r s z

| Only straight lines | Only curved lines | Both |
|---|---|---|
| | | |

**NOW TRY THIS!**

- **Write more letters of your own in the table.**

**Teachers' note** Begin by discussing the meaning of the words 'curved' and 'straight' and ask the children to write some letters of the alphabet in the air and to discuss the lines used. Encourage children to cross off each letter as they write it into the table. Encourage them to use the letters in their name and to place them correctly in the table.

**100% New Developing Mathemat** **Using and Applying Mathematics** **Ages 5–6** © A & C BLACK

# Talking shapes

- **Cut out the cards.**
- **With a friend, sort the** shapes **into groups.**

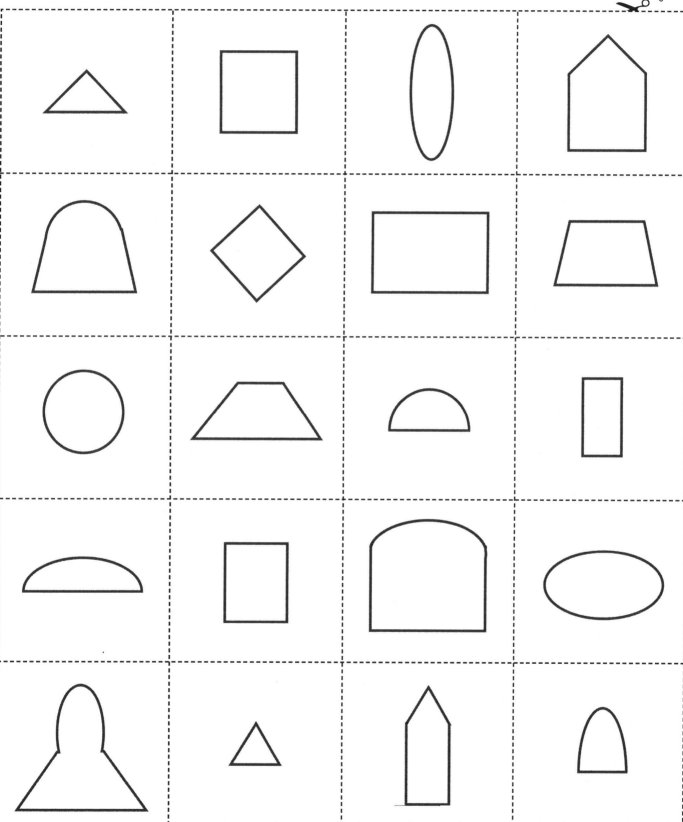

**Teachers' note** Provide one sheet per pair. Encourage the children to talk to each other about the shapes and to decide how they would like to sort them into groups. Accept any ways of sorting, encouraging the children to explain their reasoning to others. The cards could be stuck onto different pieces of paper to show the sets.

**100% New Developing Mathematics
Using and Applying Mathematics:
Ages 5–6**
© A & C BLACK

47

# Dicey dilemmas

• Draw the next [two] dice in each pattern.

Row 1:

Row 2:

Row 3:

Row 4:

Row 5:

**NOW TRY THIS!**  • Now draw a dice pattern of your own.

**Teachers' note** Begin by introducing dice and giving the children a chance to play with them and explore the patterns they notice. Explain that no two sides of a dice are identical. Ensure that children understand what a pattern is.

**100% New Developing Mathemat[ics]
Using and Applying Mathematics
Ages 5–6
© A & C BLACK**

# Domino dilemmas: 1

- **Draw the next** [two] **dominoes in each pattern.**

  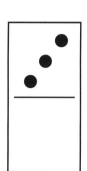   

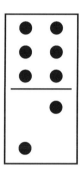   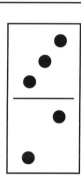  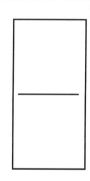

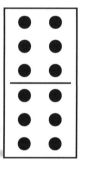 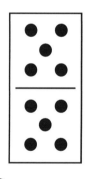  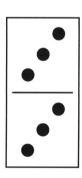  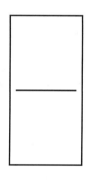

**NOW TRY THIS!**

- **Make up a domino pattern of your own.**

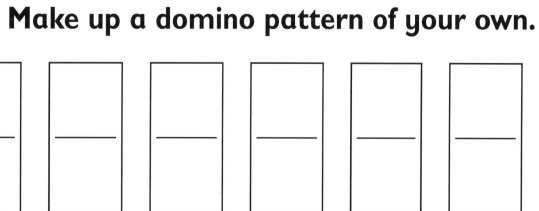

**Teachers' note** Begin by introducing dominoes and giving the children a chance to play with them and explore patterns they notice. Explain that no two dominoes are identical. The following sheet can be given as a more challenging activity.

**100% New Developing Mathematics Using and Applying Mathematics: Ages 5–6**
© A & C BLACK

**49**

- **Draw the next** two **dominoes in each pattern.**

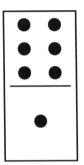     

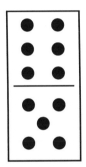 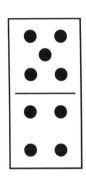  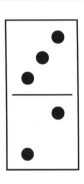 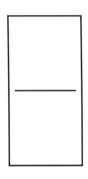 

 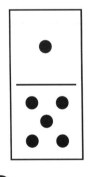  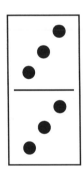  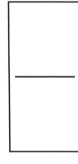

NOW TRY THIS!

- **Make up a domino pattern of your own.**

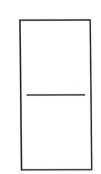    

**Teachers' note** Begin by introducing dominoes and giving the children a chance to play with them and explore patterns they notice. Explain that no two dominoes are identical. The previous sheet can be given as the introductory sheet and this one used for more challenging work.

**100% New Developing Mathematics**
**Using and Applying Mathematics**
**Ages 5–6**
© A & C BLACK

# Buckets and spades

- **Talk to a friend about each pattern and say what will come next.**

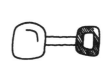

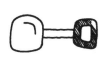

 **NOW TRY THIS!**

- **Copy one of the patterns above and continue the pattern to make it longer.**

**Teachers' note** Some children may find it easier to describe and continue the patterns by colouring all the buckets red, the flat spades blue and the upright spades green.

**100% New Developing Mathematics Using and Applying Mathematics: Ages 5–6** © A & C BLACK

# Odd tile out

- In each design, $\boxed{8}$ of the square tiles are the same. $\boxed{1}$ is different.
- Colour the odd tile out in each design.

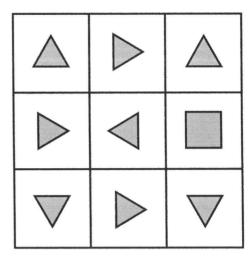

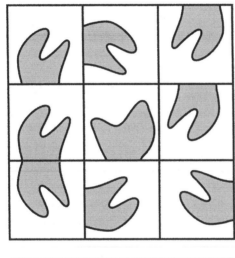

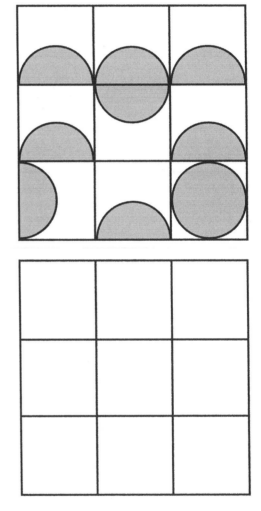

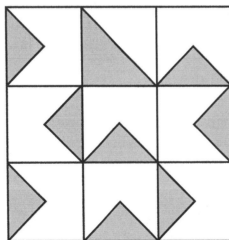

**NOW TRY THIS!**

- Make up your own 'Odd tile out' pattern. Make all the tiles the same except for one.

**Teachers' note** Introduce this activity by using 9 square tiles that are the same to make a pattern. Remove and replace one tile with a different one and explain that it is the odd tile out. Ensure that children understand that each tile can be twisted around but it is still the same tile.

**100% New Developing Mathemat**
**Using and Applying Mathematics**
**Ages 5–6**
**© A & C BLACK**

**52**

# Even flowers

- **Colour all the** $\boxed{\text{even}}$ **numbers.**

- **Talk to a friend about what you notice.**

NOW TRY THIS!

- **Where do you think the** $\boxed{\text{even}}$ **numbers will be in this flower bed?**
- **Fill in the numbers to check.**

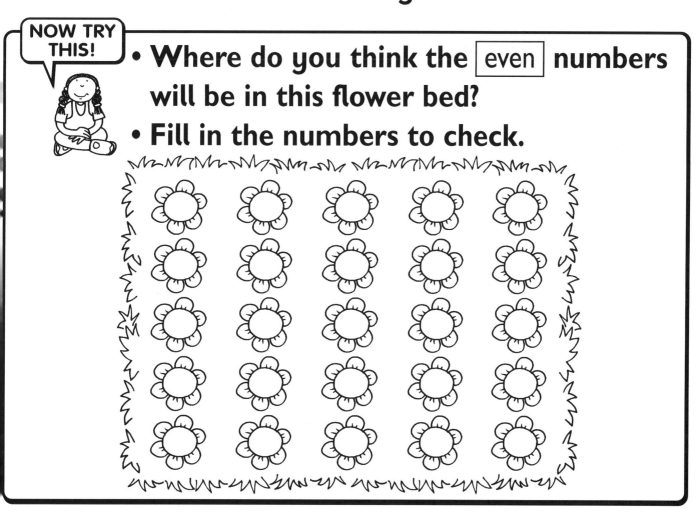

**Teachers' note** Encourage the children to describe what they notice to a partner, and introduce the vocabulary 'straight lines' and 'diagonal patterns'. Ask them to say why they think some flower beds show one type of pattern and others another, and draw attention to the number of flowers in each row.

**100% New Developing Mathematics Using and Applying Mathematics: Ages 5–6**
© A & C BLACK

# Odd, even, odd, even...

- **Find a route from the start to the outside that follows the pattern odd, even, odd, even...**
- **What is the longest route you can find?**

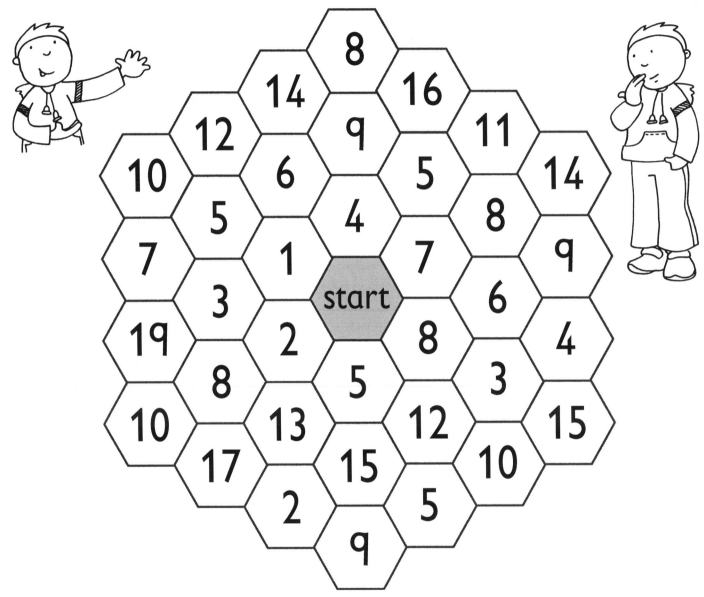

- **How many different ways can you find?**

**NOW TRY THIS!**

- **Talk to a friend about whether it is possible to find a route that uses all the numbers.**

---

**Teachers' note** Remind the children of all the odd and even numbers up to 20 and point out that the last digit of a two-digit number indicates whether it is odd or even.

**100% New Developing Mathema**
**Using and Applying Mathematic**
**Ages 5–6**
**© A & C BLACK**

# Flower power

- **Work in order.**
- **Colour <u>one</u> petal in:**

every **2nd** flower | red |
every **3rd** flower | orange |
every **4th** flower | yellow |
every **5th** flower | green |
every **6th** flower | blue |

1

2

3

4

5

6

7

8

9

10

11

12

13

14

15

16

17

18

19

20

- **Which flowers have:**

  | 4 | **colours?** _____

  **no colours?** _____

**Teachers' note** Demonstrate how to colour every second flower by saying  no, yes, no, yes, etc. and ensure that children colour one petal only of all the flowers with even numbers. Similarly, demonstrate colouring every third, fourth, fifth and sixth numbers. Encourage them to predict which flowers will be coloured more than once and to look for patterns at the end.

**100% New Developing Mathematics**
**Using and Applying Mathematics:**
**Ages 5–6**
© A & C BLACK

# Ladybird party

- Tick ☑ the ladybirds you think have exactly ⬜ dots.

- Do **not** count the dots.

- **Now count the dots. Write how many.**

**Teachers' note** Write the number 7, 8 or 9 into the box at the top according to the abilities of the children. Explain that they must tick the ladybirds that they think have exactly that number of dots. Give them a limited length of time to do this before asking them to check their predictions by counting the dots in each ladybird.

**56**

100% New Developing Mathemati
Using and Applying Mathematics
**Ages 5–6**
© A & C BLACK

# Lots or few?

- **Work with a friend.**
- **Look around your classroom and school.**
- **Collect information about things that there are:**

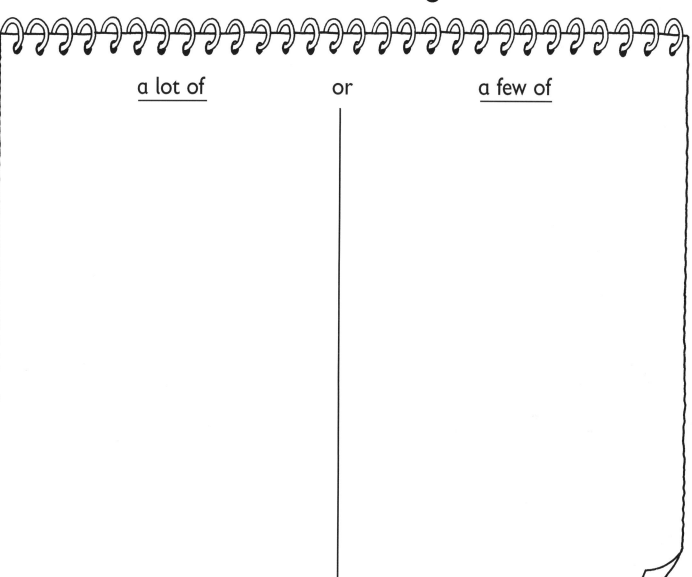

|  a lot of  |  or  |  a few of  |
|---|---|---|

**NOW TRY THIS!**

- **Look at the things that there are 'a few of'.**
- **Count roughly how many of each thing there are.**

**Teachers' note** Invite the children to suggest how many might be 'a lot' (chairs, pencils, paperclips, children) and how many might be 'a few' (teachers, waste bins). Pairs should not be told exactly how to record their answers, but instead should be encouraged to choose their own way to show the information. Some children may draw pictures, others may use writing.

**100% New Developing Mathematics
Using and Applying Mathematics:
Ages 5–6
© A & C BLACK**

# Share the cheese

A large piece of cheese must be shared between the mice family.

Mummy    Miny    Molly    Milly

Mummy mouse gets double the amount of cheese that Miny gets.

Milly and Molly get the same amount.

• **Talk to a friend about how to solve this puzzle.**
• **All the cheese must be eaten.**
• **Use this piece of cheese to help you.**

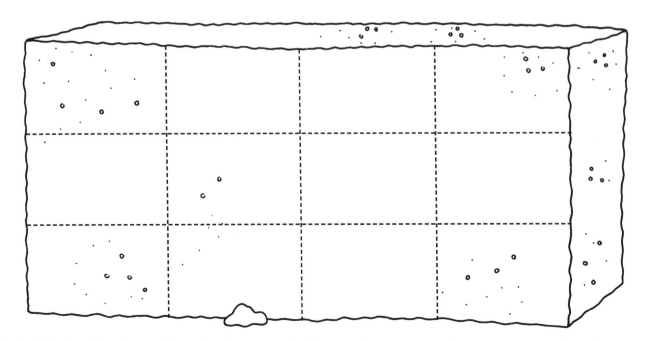

**Teachers' note** This activity focuses on thinking about how to solve a problem and using trial and improvement to solve it. Encourage the children to record their solutions on paper and discuss whether there is more than one possible answer. Provide scissors for the children to use should they need to cut up the block of cheese.

**100% New Developing Mathema**
**Using and Applying Mathematic**
**Ages 5–6**
© A & C BLACK

# Maths Challenge

- **Work in a group.**
- **Choose a task and decide how to test the question.**
- **Make sure you all agree on the rules.**
- **Now try it and record the results.**

## Task 1

Who can be the quickest to make a stick of 12 cubes?

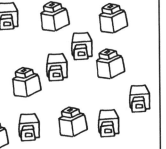

## Task 2

Who has the widest stretch from the top of their thumb to their little finger?

## Task 3

Who is nearest when estimating the number of pencils in a pencil pot?

## Task 4

Who will get the largest total when rolling a dice 6 times and adding the numbers together?

## Task 5

Who can draw the most triangles in one minute?

## Task 6

Who has the widest arm stretch between the tips of the fingers of both hands?

## Task 7

When picking 2 digit cards, who can make the largest two-digit number?

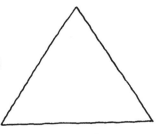

## Task 8

Who can grab and hold the most cubes in one hand without dropping them?

**Teachers' note** The children should be encouraged to make decisions about how each task could be carried out and the best way to score or record the results. Draw attention to any groups that choose to record the results in a table or list and discuss decisions made about rules or constraints.

**100% New Developing Mathematics**
**Using and Applying Mathematics:**
**Ages 5–6**
**© A & C BLACK**

# Doodlepots

- **Decorate** the pots using these **patterns**.
- **You can use** 1 **or** 2 **patterns on a pot.**
- **You cannot use all 3 patterns on a pot.**

Stripes 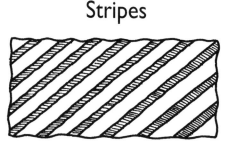    Spots 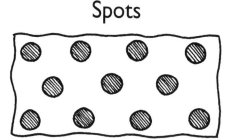    Squiggles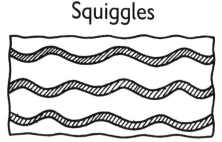

- **How many different pots can you make?** _____

**Teachers' note** Ask the children to explain their choices and to describe the decorations and differences between the pots. Invite them to notice pots that have some similarities and those that are very different. Ask children to describe why some pots have the same pattern but look different from each other, for example the spots are above the stripes here and below the stripes here.

100% New Developing Mathematics
Using and Applying Mathematics:
Ages 5–6
© A & C BLACK

# Ed the explorer

- ## Cut out Ed the explorer.

- # Put Ed so that he is touching:
  - ## a bear, a rabbit and an elephant
  - ## 2 rabbits and a bear
  - ## 2 elephants and a bear
  - ## 2 bears, a rabbit and an elephant

**Teachers' note** Children should cut out the square at the bottom to use to position Ed in different places on the grid (only touching vertically or horizontally). Encourage the children to visualise and predict which animals he touches in the different positions and to use trial and improvement strategies to find solutions. Discuss that there can be more than one solution.

**100% New Developing Mathematics Using and Applying Mathematics: Ages 5–6**
© A & C BLACK

# Balancing act

- **Work out which toy is** boxed[heaviest] **.**
- **Can you find** boxed[two] **toys that weigh the same?**

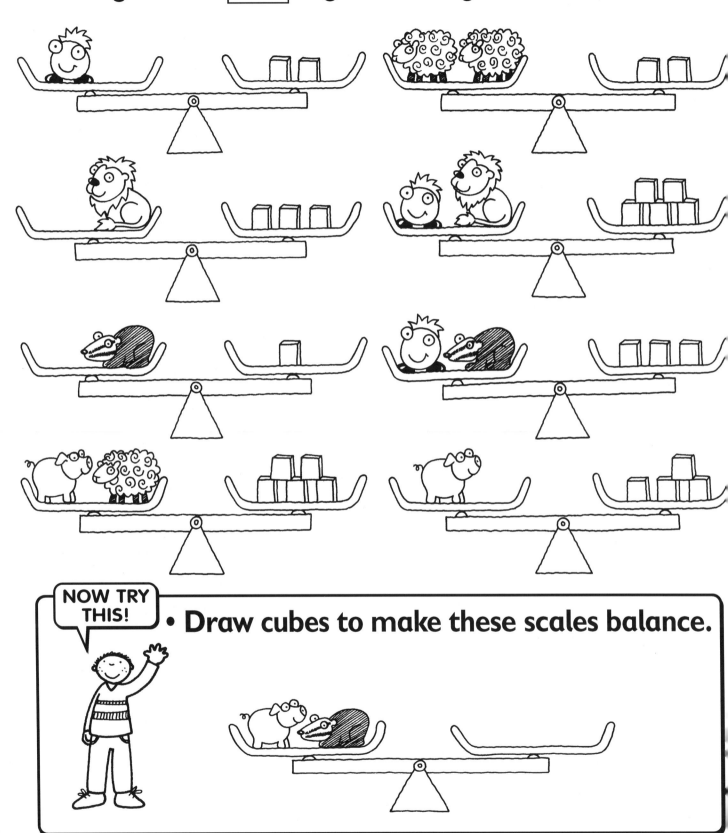

**NOW TRY THIS!**
- **Draw cubes to make these scales balance.**

**Teachers' note** Encourage the children to work in pairs to promote discussion. Ask them to find how many cubes balance each toy and, where two toys are on the scales, to check that their answers match the number of cubes shown.

**100% New Developing Mathema**
**Using and Applying Mathematic**
**Ages 5–6**
© A & C BLACK

# Ben's pets

• **Write the word** add **or** subtract .

---

Ben has 4 cats and 2 kittens.

• **How many in total?**

add

---

Ben had 5 frogs but 1 jumped away.

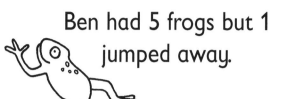

• **How many frogs now?**

---

Ben has 3 angel fish and 5 goldfish.

• **How many fish altogether?**

---

Ben has 3 more rabbits than Sam. Sam has 1 rabbit.

• **How many rabbits has Ben?**

---

Ben has 6 budgies. Sam has 4 fewer than Ben.

• **How many budgies has Sam?**

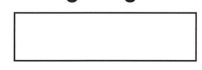

---

Ben had 7 puppies but 2 were sold.

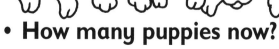
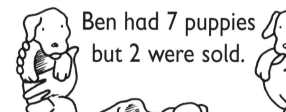

• **How many puppies now?**

---

**Teachers' note** Explain to the children that they do not need to answer the questions, but instead to think about how they would work it out using addition or subtraction. Some children could be asked to write the appropriate + and – sign and once completed the children could then answer the questions. As an extension activity, ask the children to make up their own pet questions.

**100% New Developing Mathematics
Using and Applying Mathematics:
Ages 5–6**
© A & C BLACK

# Flo's florists

- **Write the word** add **or** subtract .

---

This bunch has 3 roses
and 4 daisies.

- **How many flowers?**

---

This bunch had 8 tulips but
3 of them died.

- **How many tulips now?**

---

A piece of ribbon has 10 stars
on. Flo cuts off 4 stars.

- **How many stars are left?**

---

A vase has 3 cups of water in it.
Flo pours in 4 more cups.

- **How many cups altogether?**

---

This vase holds 12 roses.
A lady buys 4 of them.

- **How many roses now?**

---

There are 3 ladybirds on this
flower. 5 more arrive.

- **How many ladybirds now?**

---

**Teachers' note** Explain to the children that they do not need to answer the questions, but instead to think about how they would work it out using addition or subtraction. Some children could be asked to write the appropriate + and – sign and once completed the children could then answer the questions. As an extension activity, ask the children to make up their own questions.

**64**

**100% New Developing Mathema**
**Using and Applying Mathematics**
**Ages 5–6**
**© A & C BLACK**